KU-223-184

NIGHT AFTER NIGHT

Neil Bartlett

The Royal Court Writers Series published by
Methuen Drama in association with the Royal Court Theatre

Royal Court Writers Series

Night After Night was first published in Great Britain
in the Royal Court Writers Series in 1993
by Methuen Drama
an imprint of Reed Consumer Books Ltd
Michelin House, 81 Fulham Road, London SW3 6RB
in association with the Royal Court Theatre
Sloane Square, London SW1N 8AS
and distributed in the United States of America
by Heinemann, a division of Reed Publishing (USA) Inc
361 Hanover Street, Portsmouth, New Hampshire NH 03801 3959

ISBN 0–413–68500–4

A CIP catalogue record for this book
is available from the British Library

Front cover photograph by Mike Laye
Lines from *Look Back In Anger* by John Osborne quoted on page 21
by kind permission of the author and Faber & Faber Ltd

Typeset by Hewer Text Composition Services, Edinburgh
Printed and bound in Great Britain by Cox & Wyman Ltd,
Reading, Berks

Caution

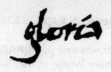

The Royal Court Theatre and Gloria present

Night After Night

book & lyrics by Neil Bartlett
music by Nicolas Bloomfield

First performance at the Traverse Theatre,
Edinburgh on 10 August 1993

First performance at the Royal Court Theatre
on 24 November 1993

Financially assisted by the Royal Borough of Kensington and Chelsea
Recipient of an Arts Council Incentive Funding Award

Recipient of a grant from the Theatre Restoration Fund &
from the Foundation for Sports & the Arts

The Royal Court's Play Development Programme is
funded by the Audrey Skirball-Kenis Theatre

Registered Charity number 231242

Night After Night is sponsored by Millivres Ltd.

Night After Night is also funded by: National Endowment for the Arts;
Rockefeller Foundation's Multi-Arts Production Fund and the Suitcase Fund;
A Project of Ideas and Means in Cross-Cultural Artist Relations; an Initiative
created by New York's Dance Theater Workshop with major funding from the
Rockefeller Foundation. Gloria is a Registered Charity No. 1021764.

   The British Council

SPONSORSHIP STATEMENT

MILLIVRES LTD - publishers of the market leading GAY TIMES magazine and Britain's longest established gay merchandising company - is proud to be associated with GLORIA THEATRE in the staging of NIGHT AFTER NIGHT.

Business sponsorship of the arts and particularly of the theatre is of increasing importance and this major new deal is the first time that MILLIVRES LTD has sponsored such a high profile theatrical event. Our involvement is in part a recognition of GLORIA's growing reputation as a producer of passionate, uncompromising theatre shows, and the level of sponsorship provided by MILLIVRES LTD confirms the belief that this new production will have a considerable impact on an international level with both gay and straight audiences.

The highly acclaimed work of GLORIA, pushing the boundaries of conventional theatre and reaching out to an ever wider audience, perfectly reflects MILLIVRES' own objectives of providing professional quality products and services which enhance our gay roots and maximise our impact both within and beyond the gay community.

This remarkable and unusual partnership between MILLIVRES and GLORIA shows that both companies, while retaining their roots firmly in the gay community in London, are fast developing a national and international profile. At a time of national recession, the partnership is a major advance for the visibility of gay and lesbian businesses.

MILLIVRES LTD is an award winner under the Business Sponsorship Incentive Scheme for its support of GLORIA's production of NIGHT AFTER NIGHT. The BSIS is a Government Scheme administered by the Association for Business Sponsorship of the Arts.

millivres ltd

Worldwide House
116-134 Bayham Street
London, NW1 0BA
Tel: 071 482 2576
Fax: 071 284 0329

1928 *Wake Up and Dream, Show Boat*

1929 *Bittersweet, Mr Cinders*

1930 *Cavalcade*

1934 *Yes, Madam?*

1935 *Anything Goes, Glamorous Night*

1936 *Careless Rapture*

1937 *Me and My Girl*

1939 *The Dancing Years*

1945 *Perchance to Dream*

1946 *Forces Showboats, Misleading Ladies*

1947 *Annie Get Your Gun, Oklahoma!, Bless The Bride*

1949 *King's Rhapsody, Brigadoon,*
The London Hippodrome Folies Bergere Revue

1950 *Carousel*

1951 *South Pacific, Zip Goes A Million*

1952 *The Merry Widow, Call Me Madam, London Laughs,*
Paris To Piccadilly

1953 *On The Town, Paint Your Wagon, Guys And Dolls,*
The King And I

1954 *Pal Joey*

1955 *The Pajama Game,*
Kismet

1957 *Bells Are Ringing*

1958 *My Fair Lady,*
West Side Story

THE ENGLISH STAGE COMPANY

The English Stage Company was formed to bring serious writing back to the stage. The Court's first Artistic Director, George Devine, wanted to create a vital and popular theatre. In order to promote this, he encouraged new writing that explored subjects drawn from contemporary life as well as pursuing European plays and forgotten classics. When John Osborne's **Look Back in Anger** was first produced in 1956, and revived in '57, it forced British Theatre into the modern age. At the same time Brecht, Giraudoux, Ionesco and Sartre were also part of the repertoire.

The ambition to discover new work which was challenging, innovative and also of the highest quality became the fulcrum of the Company's course of action. Early Court writers included Arnold Wesker, John Arden, David Storey, Ann Jellicoe, N F Simpson and Edward Bond. They were followed by a generation of writers led by David Hare and Howard Brenton, and in more recent years, celebrated house writers have included Caryl Churchill, Timberlake Wertenbaker, Robert Holman and Jim Cartwright. Many of their plays are now regarded as modern classics.

In line with the policy of nurturing new writing, the Theatre Upstairs has mainly been seen as a place for exploration and experiment, where writers learn and develop their skills prior to the demands of the Mainstage auditorium. Anne Devlin, Andrea Dunbar, Sarah Daniels, Jim Cartwright, Clare McIntyre, Winsome Pinnnock, and more recently Martin Crimp have, or will in the future, benefit from this process. The Theatre Upstairs proved its value as a focal point for new work with the production of the Chilean writer, Ariel Dorfman's **Death and the Maiden**. More recently, talented young writers as diverse as Jonathan Harvey, Adam Pernak, Phyllis Nagy (in association with the Liverpool Playhouse) and Gregory Motton (in association with the Royal National Theatre Studio) have been shown to great advantage in this space.

David Suchet and Lia Williams in **Oleanna** by David Mamet, 1993

1991, 1992, and 1993 have been record-breaking years at the box-office with capacity houses for productions of **Top Girls**, **Three Birds Alighting on a Field**, **Faith Healer**, **Death and the Maiden** (which moved to The Duke of York's), **Six Degrees of Separation** (which moved to the Comedy Theatre) and most recently **King Lear** and **Oleanna** (which has now moved to The Duke of York's). **Death and the Maiden** and **Six Degrees of Separation** won the Olivier Award for Best Play in 1992 and 1993 respectively. **Three Birds Alighting on a Field** was awarded Best West End Play by the Writer's Guild of Great Britain, and has been successfully revived.

After nearly four decades, the Royal Court Theatre is still a major focus in the country for the production of new work. Scores of plays first seen in Sloane Square are now part of the national and international dramatic repertoire.

Adrian Lester in **Six Degrees of Separation** by John Guare, 1992

Gloria is a production company set up in 1988 to produce the work of four artists: Neil Bartlett, Nicolas Bloomfield, Leah Hausman and Simon Mellor. We work together as writer/director, composer, director/choreographer and producer respectively. **Night After Night** is our tenth work for the theatre.

Our work generally takes unlikely source material - a sequence of obscure late nineteenth century paintings in **A Vision of Love Revealed in Sleep** (1989), a Balzac story about a 250 year old castrato in **Sarrasine** (1990) and a contemporary popular thriller in **A Judgement in Stone** (1992) - as the starting points for original works that have used live music and a passionate, uncompromising performance style to pursue contemporary images of sex and sexuality, power and powerlessness.

The company was set up with a very particular vision - that the differences between so-called 'difficult' work and so-called 'easy' work are more in the minds of theatre managers and marketing officers than in those of the public. In other words, we believe it is possible to create genuinely innovative theatre playing in large houses to large audiences and that our work can and must survive in the mainstream.

In 1992, the company was awarded franchise funding from the Arts Council to create five shows over the period 1992-5. **Night After Night** is the fourth of these shows. The fifth will be a new show for Nottingham Playhouse based on Oscar Wilde's **The Picture of Dorian Gray**, which will open in the Autumn of 1994. Next year **Gloria** will go into its next phase of development when the company starts a new creative partnership with the Lyric Theatre, Hammersmith.

If you want more information about the work of **Gloria**, or be the first to hear about our shows by joining our free mailing list, then please contact us: **Gloria**, 16 Chenies Street, London WC1E 7EX. Tel.: 071 636 3767 / Fax: 071 636 3653.

We would like to thank our directors, Peter Ayrton, Philip Bernays, Paul Iles, Lois Keidan and Jean Nicholson for their continuing support.

Gloria is a Registered Charity no. 1021764

Lady Audley's Secret
(1988-9)

Photo: Mike Laye

A Vision of Love Revealed in Sleep
(PART THREE)
(1989-90)

Ariadne
(1989-90)

Photo: Mike Laye

Sarrasine
(1990-1)

Let Them Call It Jazz
(1991)

Twelfth Night
(1992)

Now That It's Morning
(1992)

A Judgement in Stone
(1992)

The Game of Love and Chance
(1992-3)

Night After Night (PART ONE)
(1993)

The Royal Court and Gloria would like to thank the following:

Boy's suit made by **Michael Kennedy**; Costumes made by **Cryn Horn** with assistance from **Billy Haynes, Ute Wilde, Helen Lewis, Joy Costantinides, Lorna Robinson, Rachel Blow, Pat Walters** and **Jan McNamara** and with the good will of **Jenny Henry**; Backcloth painted by **Sue Ayres**; 1950s pram kindly loaned by **Silver Cross Ltd**; umbrellas provided by **Swaine Adeney Brigg & Sons Ltd**; **Mrs Dunnington** at Harlands of Hull for theatre tickets; **Moet & Chandon**; **Sketchley Cleaners**; cigarettes supplied by **R J Reynolds**; wig by **Derek Eason**; confetti supplied by **Deeko/A Division of Jamont (UK) Ltd; Liz Reed; Donna Comfort; Sarah Travis; Sara Hamill; Nick Bloom; Chris O'May; Kenneth McEwan; Simon Fanshawe; Kevin Sollis; Greater London Pianos; Penny Johns; London Contemporary Dance School**; all the staff at **Dance Theatre Workshop, Drill Hall Arts Centre, New York Shakespeare Festival, National Performance Network, On The Boards, Royal Court Theatre, Traverse Theatre, Walker Art Center** and **Union Chapel**.

Wardrobe care by Persil and Comfort; watches by The Timex Corporation; refrigerators by Electrolux and Philips Major Appliances Ltd.; kettles for rehearsals by Morphy Richards; video for casting purposes by Hitachi; backstage coffee machine by West 9; furniture by Knoll International; freezer for backstage use supplied by Zanussi Ltd 'Now that's a good idea.' Hair by Carole at Edmond's, 19 Beauchamp Place, SW3. Thanks to Casio for use of DAT equipment; closed circuit TV cameras and monitors by Mitsubishi UK Ltd. Natural spring water from Wye Spring Water, 149 Sloane Street, London SW1, tel. 071-730 6977. Overhead projector from W.H. Smith. The London Trophy Company, 653 Holloway Road, N19, 071 272 6245.

Night After Night

book & lyrics	**Neil Bartlett**
music	**Nicolas Bloomfield**

THE CAST

Neil Bartlett

Beverley Klein

Reginald S Bundy

Craig Deegan

Paul Shaw

Stephen Speed

François Testory

THE BAND

violin/percussion	**Anna Hemery**
saxophone/clarinet	**Shaun Thompson**
	Dai Pritchard
double bass	**Andrew Cruickshank**
piano	**Nicolas Bloomfield**

Producer	**Simon Mellor**
Director	**Neil Bartlett**
Musical Director	**Nicolas Bloomfield**
Choreographer	**Leah Hausman**
Costume Designers	**Cryn Horn**
	Neil Bartlett
Lighting Designer	**David Kavanagh**
Production Manager	**David Kavanagh**
DSM	**Cassie Arundel**
ASM	**Billy Haynes**
Company Administrator	**Mavis Seaman**
Company Accountant	**Carole Dale**
Office Intern	**Dac Panitpakdi**
Publicity Photography	**Mike Laye**
Production Photography	**Sean Hudson**
Publicity Design	**Roy Trevelion**
Royal Court Leaflet	**Loft**

ACT ONE
Overture

6.40pm: The Foyer "Waiting" ....*Neil Bartlett*

The Box Office ....*Nicolas Bloomfield*

The Cloakroom ....*Reginald Bundy*

The Opening of the House ....*Craig Deegan*

The Dress Circle Bar ....*Paul Shaw*

The Programmes: "When Two People Meet"............*François Testory*

The Tickets: "There You Are" ....*Stephen Speed*

7.29pm: The Stage "Places Please" ....*Beverley Klein & The Boys*

There will be one interval of 15 minutes

ACT TWO

"You Gotta Have Conviction".................*Reginald Bundy & The Boys*

"Those West End Nights" ....
......................................*François Testory, Craig Deegan & Stephen Speed*

"Set Your Life To Music".......................................*Paul Shaw*

"Anywhere But Here" ....*The Company*

"Tell Me How You'd Like Me" ....*Beverley Klein*

"Life Could Be Wonderful" ....*Beverley Klein & Craig Deegan*

"There's Nothing In The Way": ballet ....
....*François Testory, Stephen Speed & The Boys*

"No-one Knows" ....*Beverley Klein*

7.30pm: "Finale"

The action takes place in a theatre in the West End of London, one night during the early spring of 1958.

No time elapses between the end of the first Act and the start of the second.

BIOGRAPHIES

CASSIE ARUNDEL

For the Royal Court: Zoetrope (Young People's Theatre at the Commonwealth Institute); Night After Night (Part One) (with Gloria). For Gloria: A Judgement in Stone. Other stage management work includes: Beyond Belief (London Small Theatre Company); The Hobbit, The Last Gamble, On The Piste (Upstart Productions); Ines De Castro (Traverse Theatre Production at the Riverside); Brand (Aldwych & tour). Four years as resident stage manager at the Latchmere, Battersea.

NEIL BARTLETT

Performer, director, translator, writer and founder member of Gloria.
For the Royal Court: Night After Night (Part One) (with Gloria). For Gloria: Lady Audley's Secret, A Vision of Love Revealed in Sleep, Sarrasine, Let Them Call It Jazz, A Judgement in Stone, The Game of Love and Chance (with Cambridge Theatre Co. and Royal National Theatre).
Other theatre work includes: More Bigger Snacks Now (Complicite); The Misanthrope (Red Shift & Goodman Theatre, Chicago); Berenice (Royal National Theatre); School for Wives (Derby Playhouse & Arena Stage, Washington); The Avenging Woman (Riga & Toronto); Twelfth Night (Goodman Theatre, Chicago). Film, TV and video work includes:

That's What Friends are For, Where is Love, Pedagogue (with Stuart Marshall), That's How Strong My Love Is, Now That It's Morning. Published works include: Who Was That Man?, Berenice/The Misanthrope/School For Wives, The Game Of Love And Chance, A Vision of Love Revealed in Sleep, Ready To Catch Him Should He Fall. Neil Bartlett is Artistic Director Designate of the Lyric Theatre, Hammersmith.

NICOLAS BLOOMFIELD

Composer, arranger, performer and member of Gloria. Trained at the Royal Academy of Music.
For the Royal Court: Night After Night (Part One) (with Gloria). For Gloria: Lady Audley's Secret, Ariadne, A Vision of Love Revealed in Sleep, Sarrasine, A Judgement in Stone, The Game of Love and Chance (with Cambridge Theatre Co. and Royal National Theatre), Now That It's Morning. Other musical direction for the theatre includes: Dressing Up (Cockpit); The Magic Flute (ICA); Mahagonny Songspiel (Oxford); Alice in Wonderland (Albany Empire); Dull Morning, Cloudy Mild (Jonathan Burrows/Matteo Farjeon) and Looking Behaviour (Liz Ranken/Phil Griffin). Other composition for the theatre includes: Edward II (Media Show), Resurrection (Nigel Charnock); Twelfth Night (Goodman Theatre, Chicago).

REGINALD S BUNDY

For Gloria: A Vision of Love Revealed in Sleep, Now That It's Morning.
Other theatre includes: Fiddler on the Roof (original West End production), Elegies for Angels, Punks and Raging Queens (Criterion) and seasons at the London Palladium, Queens, Roundhouse, Westcliffe-on-Sea and Yvonne Arnaud theatres as well as with The Bloolips Theatre Company.
Cabaret work with the Disapointer Sisters and his solo act, Regina Fong, Last of the Romanoffs (performed in London and at the Edinburgh Festival).

ANDREW CRUICKSHANK

Freelance musician. Trained at the Royal Academy of Music and Guildhall School of Music and Drama.
For Gloria: Sarrasine, A Judgement in Stone.
Other companies, bands and orchestras worked with include: The Philarmonia, the New Queens Hall Orchestra, The Scottish Chamber Orchestra, The Orchestra of St John's Smith Square, The London Classical Players, The Orchestra of the Age of Enlightenment, the London Sinfonietta, Acrobats of Desire and Glyndebourne Opera.

CRAIG DEEGAN

Trained at the Guildford School of Acting and the London Studio Centre.

Theatre includes: See-Saw, Cinderella (Northampton Royal Theatre); Cabaret, Rosencrantz and Guildenstern are Dead (Salisbury Playhouse); Aladdin (City Varieties, Leeds); Mother Goose (Theatre Royal, Drury Lane); Hair (Broadway Theatre Company, European tour); The King and I (Sadler's Wells and national tour); Snow White (Dartford Orchard); Pirates of Penzance, The Rocky Horror Show, The Broadway Show (national tours). Also appeared at the Istanbul Festival.

Radio includes: Friday Night is Music Night (with the Rob Mitchell Singers).

LEAH HAUSMAN

Director, choreographer, performer and founder member of Gloria. Trained at The American Ballet Theatre School, The Martha Graham School for Dance and Ecole Jacques Lecoq in Paris.

For Gloria: Lady Audley's Secret, Ariadne, Sarrasine, A Judgement in Stone, The Game of Love and Chance (with Cambridge Theatre Co. and Royal National).

Other theatre includes: The Magic Flute (ICA); Mahagonny Songspiel (Oxford); Whale (David Glass & Peta Lily); The Phantom Violin (Theatre de Complicite); Lamentations of Thel (Theatre de Complicite for Almeida Music

Festival); Gianni Schicchi, The Mikado, Ariadne Auf Naxos, Der Rosenkavalier (English National Opera); Pope Joan (English National Opera's Baylis Programme); Samson & Delilah (Northern Opera); Twelfth Night (Goodman Theatre, Chicago).

WILLIAM HAYNES

Trained at Central School of Speech and Drama.

Stage management includes seasons at the Bush, Stowe Opera, Grand Opera House, York.

ANNA HEMERY

Freelance musician and composer. Studied at Dartington College of Arts and the Royal Academy of Music.

For Gloria: A Judgement in Stone

Other work in the theatre includes: Carmen the Play - Spain 1936 (Communicado Theatre Co); The Taming of the Shrew (RSC); Old King Cole (Leeds Playhouse); My Mother Said I Never Should (Chichester Festival Theatre); Jane Eyre (Sheffield Crucible); School for Wives, Wind in the Willows, A Midsummer Night's Dream, Baby Doll, Trelawney of the Wells (Royal National Theatre).

Regularly plays with orchestras including: East of England, English String and Welsh Chamber.

Bands worked with include: Squeeze; Rip, Rig and Panic; Fun Boy Three; Acrobats of Desire.

CRYN HORN

Freelance costume cutter.

Theatre work includes: The Lyceum, Edinburgh, Tyneside Theatre, Newcastle, Citizens' Theatre, Glasgow, Royal National Theatre, Drill Hall (Dramatix pantomimes). Other work has included costume making for revues and the BBC's By the Sword Divided.

DAVID KAVANAGH

Production Manager and Lighting Designer. Studied at Leeds University.

For Gloria: Lady Audley's Secret, Ariadne, A Vision of Love Revealed in Sleep, Sarrasine, Let Them Call It Jazz, A Judgement in Stone, The Game of Love and Chance (with Cambridge Theatre and Royal National Theatre).

Other theatre production management work includes: National Revue of Live Art, Bloolips, Liz Ranken, Union 212, The Drill Hall Arts Centre, The Pontorson Arts Festival, Normandy, France.

BEVERLEY KLEIN

For The Royal Court: The Woman Who Cooked Her Husband (with Snarling Beasties).

For Gloria: Sarrasine, A Judgement in Stone, Now That's It's Morning.

Other theatre includes: Les Miserables (RSC & Palace); Stevie (Watermill); Educating Rita (Gateway, Chester); The Bald Prima Donna, The Breasts of Tiresias and The Winter's Tale

(Crucible, Sheffield); Stags and Hens (Dukes, Lancaster); Talent, Torch Song Trilogy (Library, Manchester); Mirandolina (Bristol Old Vic); Macbeth (Nuffield, Southampton), Carousel (Royal Exchange, Manchester), Fiddler on the Roof (Wimbledon Theatre & national tour); A Little Night Music (Wolsley, Ipswich); The Threepenny Opera (Scottish Opera); Tatyana, A Big Night Out at Little Sands Picture Palace (Nottingham Playhouse); You Never Know Who's Out There (Drill Hall); Fiddler on the Roof (West Yorkshire Playhouse).
TV includes: Absolutely, Hale and Pace, Came Out it Rained Went Back In Again, Inspector Morse, The Bill.

SIMON MELLOR

Producer and founder member of Gloria.
For Gloria: producer of all shows. Has also worked with: Pegasus Theatre, Oxford (Director), Battersea Arts Centre (Education Officer), Theatre de Complicite, The South Bank Centre, Drill Hall, Wissel Theatre, Abel & Gordon (Belgium).

DAI PRITCHARD

Freelance musician. Studied at Trinity College and the National Centre for Orchestral Studies. Theatre includes: Assassins (Donmar); West Side Story; Cabaret.
Bands and orchestras worked with include: Loose Tubes, Billy

Jenkin's Voice of God Collective, Stan Tracey's Big Band, Django Bates' Powder Room Collapse Orchestra and Delightful Precipice, The Almeida Ensemble, Gemini, Phoenix Saxophone Quartet, Harmonie Band, the Kippers.

MAVIS SEAMAN

Administrator.
Previously worked with: Citizens' Theatre, Glasgow, The Arts/ Unicorn Theatre, Leeds Playhouse, Bush Theatre, ICA, Royal Court, Drill Hall. Co-director of the Pontorson Arts Festival, Normandy.

PAUL SHAW.

Theatre includes: Lust in Space, Vamp and Camp, Gland Motel, Get Hur, Living leg-ends (Bloolips, as performer, designer and writer). Trained as Theatre Designer at Wimbledon School of Art and has worked as assistant director at the Citizens' Theatre, Glasgow.

STEPHEN SPEED

Trained at the Royal Ballet School. Theatre includes: Peter Pan; Little; Cunning Little Vixen (Royal Opera); Peter Pan, Hans Anderson (national tours). Member of the Royal Ballet for five years where he worked with choreographers including Sir Kenneth MacMillan, Sir Frederick Ashton and Leonide Massine. Has spent seasons with English National Opera, The New Shakespeare Company,

Tynewear Theatre Company and Theatre Royal, York.
TV includes: The Two Ronnies, Dr Who, The House of Elliott.

FRANÇOIS TESTORY

Trained at MUDRA.
For Gloria: Sarrasine, Now That It's Morning.
Other theatre includes: Orpheus in the Underworld (English National Opera); Phedre (Royal Opera House); Taylor of Gloucester (Sadlers Wells); Nephelim (Sogetsu Hall, Tokyo); Smoking Mirror (Celestino-Coronado, Alfredo Cordal), Salome (Parco Theatre, Tokyo), Sylano Bussotti (Bologna), Von Magnet (Paris), Luca Mainardi (London). He performs his own singing cabaret entitled L'Amande Amere.

SHAUN THOMPSON

Freelance musician. Studied at trinity College and the National Centre for Orchestral Studies.
For Gloria: A Judgement in Stone. Other Theatre includes: A Winter's Tale, Angels in America (Royal National Theatre),; Carmen Jones (Old Vic); Comedy of Errors (RSC); Crazy for You (Prince Edward's).
Orchestras played with include: London Symphony Orchestra, The Philarmonia, the BBC Concert Orchestra, BBC Welsh Symphony Orchestra, Ulster Orchestra.

Night After Night

has taken eight months to make. The first version of the material was a solo show for Neil Bartlett, with Nicolas Bloomfield at the piano, which was performed in Edinburgh, New York and London in January and February 1993. This has been reworked to create the show you now see.

Photo: Mike Laye

This lengthy working process has only been made possible by the unswerving support shown us by our co-producers: Dance Theater Workshop (New York), The New York Shakespeare Festival, On The Boards (Seattle), The Royal Court Theatre (London), Traverse Theatre (Edinburgh) and Walker Art Center (Minneapolis).

THE OLIVIER BUILDING APPEAL

The Royal Court reached the ripe old age of 100 in September 1988. The theatre was showing its age somewhat, and the centenary was celebrated by the launch of the Olivier Appeal, for £800,000 to repair and improve the building.

Laurence Olivier's long association with the Court began as a schoolboy. He was given "a splendid seat in the Dress Circle" to see his first Shakespeare, **Henry IV Part 2** *and was later to appear as Malcolm in* **Macbeth** *(in modern dress) in a Barry Jackson production, visiting from the Birmingham Repertory Theatre in 1928. His line of parts also included the Lord in the Prologue of* **The Taming of the Shrew**. *This early connection and his astonishing return in* **The Entertainer**, *which changed the direction of his career in 1957, made it natural that he should be the Appeal Patron. After his death, Joan Plowright CBE, the Lady Olivier, consented to take over as Patron.*

We are now three-quarters of the way to our target. With the generous gifts of our many friends and donors, and an award from the Arts Council's Incentive Fund, we have enlarged and redecorated the bars and front of house areas, installed a new central heating boiler and new air conditioning equipment in both theatres, rewired many parts of the building, redecorated the dressing rooms and we are gradually upgrading the lighting and sound equipment.

With the help of the Theatre Restoration Fund, work has now been completed on building a rehearsal room and replacing the ancient roofs. The Foundation for Sport and the Arts has promised a grant which will enable us to restore the faded Victorian facade of the theatre. So, much is being done, but much remains to do, to improve the technical facilities backstage which will open up new possibilities for our set designers.

Can you help? A tour of the theatre, including its more picturesque parts, can be arranged by ringing Becky Shaw on 071 730 5174. If you would like to help with an event or a gift please ring Graham Cowley, General Manager, on the same number.

Laurence Olivier 1907-1989
Photo: Snowdon

'Secure the Theatre's future, and take it forward towards the new century. For the health of the whole theatrical life of Britain it is essential that this greatly all-providing theatre we love so much and wish so well continues to prosper.'
Laurence Olivier (1988)

THE ROYAL COURT THEATRE

Persons shall not be permitted to stand or sit in any of the gangways intersecting the seating or sit in any of the other gangways. The Management reserves the right to refuse admission and to make any alterations in the cast which may be rendered necessary by illness or other unavoidable causes.
Patrons are reminded that smoking is not permitted in the auditorium or the Stalls Bar. No photographs to be taken or tape recordings to be made.

Night After Night

Preface

> 'People used to say to each other, they'd say, you know, so-and-so, he's "musical".'
>
> From a conversation with a chorus boy

Some people think that performers in the theatre mean what they say, and only what they say. According to this theory, gay people only really started to appear on stage in Britain in the late 1960s and 'gay theatre' is a series of plays in which people talk about the 'theme' or 'subject' of homosexuality. Before that (so the theory goes), all we had was a few tortured ancestors – the frightened or frightening queens of *The Vortex*, *The Green Bay Tree*, the Britten operas, *Cat On A Hot Tin Roof*. True, some of the most famous, glamorous and successful authors on the West End stage were (unknown to their public) homosexual – Coward, Rattigan, Maugham, Novello – but they never said what they really wanted to say, and so must be consigned to our pre-history.

This version of history chooses to forget that gay people were there all the time, occupying a central place in the manufacture of all our nights out – stage managing, dressing, selling the tickets, directing, designing, composing and choreographing the most popular shows in town. One particular kind of artist has always worked right in the heart of the West End: the chorus boy. Applauded, desirable, skilful, athletic, he contradicted and contradicts every stereotype of a gay person. The strange thing is that he does it without saying a word, and whilst dancing his way through lyrics and plots that have, or ought to have, absolutely nothing to do with the reality of our lives.

This conundrum persists: thousands of people go to see shows every night and have no idea that they are watching their fantasies being acted out by gay people, while gay people still know what they have always known, that shows which 'say' nothing about us can still be some of the most powerful and exciting vehicles of our pleasures and our griefs.

Night After Night started with an anecdote: my father's memories of a visit to the West End in 1958 made me wonder about the differences (and similarities) between his nights out and mine. When that curtain rises and those lights go down, whose dreams are these shows actually orchestrating? I think this question is a much larger one than simply why a man like him might enjoy watching the chorus boys of a musical (without knowing what they really were) or why men like me enjoy the same musicals as he did (knowing that we should know better). What is it about the way musicals treat possibility, certainty, memory and vision that makes such different people ('all kinds of people') remember them so well and look forward to them so much?

Characters

The characters who appear in **Night After Night** are, with the exception of Trevor Bartlett, unnamed. This reflects the fact that they are types, anecdotes or quotations as much as they are people. In the script they are referred to either by their role at any particular moment or by the first name of the performer. This naming reflects the fact that quite often in the performance deliberate use is made of the confusion or similarity between character and performer.

The Script

The spoken text of **Night After Night** was almost completely re-written and re-distributed during rehearsals and the first month of performances so that it reflected more accurately not only the speech-patterns but also the personalities and concerns of the performers for whom it was specifically written. Much of the original text was also derived from interviews with the cast, with ex-West End theatre workers and with Pam and Trevor Bartlett. This published text is, therefore, not entirely the property of the author.

Neil Bartlett, 1993

Sources for the text of **Night After Night** include: popular fiction of the 1950s (*The Charioteer, A Chorus of Witches, The Painted King, The Heart in Exile*); the many West End plays, both high- and low-brow, which formed the popular image of the gay man at that time

(*A Streetcar Named Desire*, *Wish You Were Here*, *Serious Charge*, *No Concern Of Mine*, *Variations On A Theme* and *Five Finger Exercise*); such unlikely items of period ephemera as: period ads from the back of *Plays and Players*; ads for Vince Green swimwear and an article by Barbara Cartland written for the *Sunday Pictorial* in 1952 entitled 'These Evil Men'.

Act One

The stage is empty: all the musical instruments, music stands, microphones, props etc. required for the show are there, but look more like an abandoned jumble of objects than the set for a musical. This setting never really changes; the whole show is accomplished with six gilt chairs and two costume rails. All the locations are created by the choreography, all the costume changes done either onstage or behind the costume rails; the impression is created that no one ever goes off. Only during the ballet does the black, empty back wall dissolve to reveal a full technicolour setting. All the costumes are in the extreme colours of a 1950s filmed musical: blacks, dark blues, reds, yellows, oranges, pinks.

Neil *and* **Nicolas** *enter, dressed identically.* **Neil** *sits and listens to Overture, on a solo piano.*

During the Overture, five empty chairs are filled by five figures who appear to be identical to **Neil***: dinner suits, bow ties, short back-and-sides.* **Neil** *sits and listens to the music. Suddenly he stands.*

Neil Good evening. Good evening.

Sometimes, when people see me for the first time they say: Good heavens. It can't be. It can't be him. It couldn't possibly be him.

That's because sometimes, at family gatherings, people mistake me for my father. They come up to me and say, do you know, I walked in and I thought it was Trevor. I thought you were your father. You look just like him. (**Neil** *dresses up as* **Trevor**.)

Good evening. My name is Trevor Bartlett. I was born in 1928. Recently married, almost four years ago exactly. No, no children. Well, not yet anyway.

I was sixteen when the war ended and then did my National Service of course. We met in '51, started courting in '52. Now you have to remember that in those days coming up into town, seeing the West End with all its lights on again, well that was a night out for us in itself.

I was working at Clapham, so used to get the train to Victoria from the Junction and then walk in, and she was working just off Portman Square and so could walk in to meet me; the point of which is that neither of us needed to take a bus, which mattered, because we were saving to get married.

We usually used to arrange to meet at the Quality Inn on Shaftesbury Avenue, because of the coffee. You paid just the once, you see. You went in and sat on a high stool at a counter, American style, and when you had finished your first coffee the waitress would simply say, Excuse me, sir, would madam like a second cup? Then we would usually just go window shopping. Late night shopping on Oxford Street was Thursdays and she'd choose things, and I'd promise myself that one day we'd have them all.

And now – well, when you're first married you don't go out so often – not least because you're still saving. But when she told me – well, when she told me that I am going to be a father, I thought, I know we should be saving, I know we've got the future to think of, but let's make tonight a special occasion –

The Box Office Queen: **Nicolas**.

Nicolas Yes, sir, and how can I help you?

Trevor Yes, I wonder, do you have any seats available for – this evening's performance?

Nicolas Tickets available Rear Stalls, Upper Circle and Balcony.

Trevor And how much are the tickets in the stalls?

Nicolas Fifteen shillings, twelve shillings or nine shillings and sixpence.

Trevor In which case could I please have –

Nicolas Single?

Trevor No. No, I'm not single.

Nicolas That's two seats Balcony evening performance early spring of 1958 House Opens seven o'clock Curtain Up seven thirty Nineteen shillings Thank you.

Trevor Thank you. (*Chords.*)

Twenty to seven. I wanted to get here early to make sure of getting tickets; it's a very popular show – I know she's going to love it. The cloakroom isn't open yet.

Standing here like this reminds me of other occasions – you know, before we met – well, it's the first thing you do when you're a young man, isn't it, up in town on National Service – you meet a girl, you buy her dinner, you take her to a show . . . I can remember that feeling, that feeling of . . . waiting:

Music: 'Waiting'.

> Getting a haircut, putting on a jacket
> Getting the train, getting the tickets, and then
> You don't know why you're waiting
> You just know there's something, or someone
> Know that there is something that you've been waiting for.
> It may be just a dream, of course
> A day-dream, maybe –
> You've so many nights ahead, so many shows in town to see! –
> And it's exciting, just the waiting
> The waiting to meet 'someone' –
> Wondrin' – is the one that you've been waiting for – all these
>   nights
> Then you start to wonder
> How it's going to be
> Is this just somebody
> It could be anybody
> Is this just another show –
> We'll see . . .
> How will I know?
> How will you know . . . Well, hell
> I guess you'll just know

And then, when you're first married you get used to being together – but you know, when you do arrange to meet up for a show, after work, like this – God, I feel like I'm courting, look at me, standing here in the foyer all dressed up and once again, I'm waiting

> For that special someone
> Though now of course you know that this is the one that you

were waiting for all those nights –
But still you start to imagine
How it's gonna be.
We've got our whole lives ahead, just you wait and see
And though you've found your someone

Craig
And though you've found your someone
Even though you're sure
Still you find you're waiting –
Waiting for that someone
Just waiting 'til she walks in through that door . . .

Neil *moves out of the spotlight which has illuminated* **Trevor** *and his romantic outburst, leaving* **Trevor***'s costume lying in the spot on the floor.*

Neil You have to remember that this is my father talking. It isn't me. It couldn't be, it couldn't be me talking about how I feel sometimes when I'm waiting to meet 'someone', it couldn't be, it couldn't possibly be because . . . this is the early spring of 1958 and I wasn't born until the autumn of that year; and it couldn't be me, because if I was arranging to meet someone in the West End of London, then I don't think this would be the show we'd choose, I mean it's a musical, strictly boy meets girl –

Stephen Good evening, this is your half hour call, gentlemen of the chorus, this is your half hour call. Thank you.

Neil – and it couldn't be me, because if I was meeting someone in the West End of London, then I don't think I would arrange to meet them at twenty to seven. The place is practically deserted. The foyer's empty. There's no one here, except my father – oh, and the man who sold him the tickets –

Music.

and the man who is just about to open the cloakroom –

Music completes under:

excuse me, excuse could I please –

The Cloakroom Queen: **Reg**. *Each of the Foyer Queens is identified by an object:* **Reg** *has a coathanger and a cloakroom ticket.*

Cloakroom Queen You meet all kinds of people, working here. Get themselves all dressed up. I feel a bit of a fool dressed like this, actually, especially on matinees, well it never seems quite right by daylight this sort of thing, does it? Two by two, up those stairs they go and muggins here is left holding the coats, all dressed up and nowhere to go at half past three in the afternoon. Still, that's life, isn't it. Some people get themselves all dressed up for their big night out, up to town and up those stairs, they get exactly what they were expecting and exactly what they paid for, and then back home on the train.

Which is lovely . . . for some people. Some people I know wouldn't mind living up there. Or at least stopping the night, if you see what I mean. Some people I know get dressed up and go out every single night, looking for that special occasion. Some people I know spend a great deal of their time waiting. And I mean years. Still – (*He hangs up Trevor's coat.*)

– I sometimes think everyone is waiting . . .
For the show to start.

Music.

Trevor I wonder, I wonder could you tell me what time does the house actually –

Cloakroom Queen Seven o'clock and (*Sings.*) there you are, sir.

Trevor Thank you very much. Seven o'clock.

Stephen Stand by for the House Opening. Stand by for House Opening.

The Front of House Manager: **Craig**. *During his speech, which he addresses to the audience as if they were all the ushers standing by to take their places,* **Reg** *makes unsuitable comments. He has heard this speech many times. Other people may also misbehave behind* **Craig's** *back.* **Trevor** *is frozen, looking at his watch.*

Front of House If I could have your attention please –

Cloakroom Oh, God, she's vile this one, I worked with him when I was at the Old Vic . . . etc.

Front of House If I could have – Reginald Bundy! – thank you.

As you are well aware, this is something we do every night of the
week except Sundays, however, for members of the general public it
remains a special occasion, therefore, ONE!:
'All members of the theatre staff will be smartly dressed at all
times.'
TWO!
'All members of the general public will be addressed as SIR and
MADAM at all times' and
THREE!
'In the unlikely event of it becoming necessary to remove any
undesirable persons from the premises I am to be informed at once.'
As I trust they can tell from our efforts to make them feel at home
here this building is intended for the use of the general public and
not for the use of anyone else. At any time. Now if you would all
take your places please – (*They all take their places.*)
The house will open tonight at seven o'clock precisely, as on every
other night . . .

Thank you.

Everyone moves. The house is opened and **Craig** *greets actual members of the
audience, as if the audience were starting to come into the auditorium.*

Good evening, sir. Good evening, madam, etc.

Good evening, sir . . . (*He spots a couple of queens.*)

Reg Good evening, sir, and are you two together? I'll put both your
coats on the one hanger, shall I?

Craig (*to* **Trevor**) And can I help you, sir?
The Dress Circle Bar, sir?
(*Sings.*) Well (*Music.*)

Neil The Dress Circle Bar is at the top of the stairs

Craig (*sings*) The second left and

Reg, **Craig** (*sing*) There you are.

Cloakroom Queen Oh, you're cutting it a bit fine . . .

Vince the Barman: **Paul**, *late of course, changing into waistcoat and identity
bracelet. He has a little table with glasses, ice bucket and ice, gin, tonic, lemon
slices, etc.*

Stephen Gentlemen of the chorus, the house is now open. The house is now open.

Vince the Barman (*sings*)
> You wonder why you're waiting, waiting for that someone,
> Wondering where they've got to, then suddenly
> There you are – (*End music.*)

Oh, you didn't half make me jump. The bar will be open in just a moment, sir. Seven o'clock. Oh, shit, it is seven.

Now what can I do you for, sir?

One gin and tonic. Certainly, sir, that'll be one and six and could I just say, sir, you've made a very wise choice – the show I mean. Lovely show, lovely music. I loved it, quite swept away I was. Still, that's the thing with your musicals isn't it? Always promising you things you can't have. Still, lovely just to have them for two hours and five minutes including interval, that's what I always say. There you are –

Offers him the gin. **Vince** *takes advantage of the fact that dramatic convention dictates that during these scenes between* **Trevor** *and the staff* **Trevor** *has to remain silent while they speak their minds for a moment in order to have a restorative little sip of gin.*

Oh, no, but it does help. Because none of us are getting any younger, are we? Makes you think. And with this job, of course, you've got time to, once they're all in and that curtain's gone up. And you have got to think, haven't you? About the future. Suicide.

No really, I think so, the thing is, I've been reading this book, very moving it is, four chapters I've got through already with this show, I think they could afford to cut just the one number if you don't mind me saying so, sir – and the thing is, it does seem that according to popular fiction suicide is the most likely outcome. Or your violent death. Or prison, of course, but I don't know about you, I don't fancy prison really. The thing is, apparently, driven by abnormal and irresistible urges, haunted by the twin spectres of exposure and humiliation, rendered incapable of love by the scars of bitterness except of course for a brief affair with an ex-member of the armed forces, well, in the end, it's bound to happen, isn't it? I mean there are some of your more socially elevated characters like your doctors and lawyers and such who people like me do meet at parties who don't like to talk about it quite so much, and of course they are, well actually, you see, I wouldn't say that they are happy . . . but they have come to terms with the, you know, situation and that's wonderful. No, hats off girls, I do think that's wonderful for them but, the thing is, you see, I've never really seen myself as the leading man type, I'm more of a character part really, and as a friend of mine said to me the other week, you never really worry about whether the chorus are happy or not, do you, and I thought that was a very true thing to say. Because it doesn't last, does it? Not for us, not that I'm saying that I haven't had, you know, acquaintances in my life, and as you know I've got my own flat now, but the thing is, working in the theatre as I do, it is very difficult to maintain a normal social life, not that I'm saying we never get an evening off because we do and that's lovely because it gives you a chance to go and see some of the other shows – usually musicals, I prefer myself. This friend I was telling you about, he said to me the other night, he said you look just the musical type and I said, well, it's funny you should say that, although the other week I fancied a change and I did go and see a more dramatic piece. I don't know if any of you saw it, it was that Streetcar with Miss Leigh. *Streetcar Named Desire*, oh, what a fabulous title. Oh, and she was fabulous in it, I thought, although I know some people thought otherwise, but I must say, and there you are, you see, I'm sorry to keep on harping on the, you know, subject, but the kindness of strangers is all very well, thank you, but Miss Leigh's husband in *Streetcar Named Desire*, what happened to him? Yes? I don't think they're following this.

Reg They wouldn't know who (**Reg** *names a different musical comedy star each night.*) is . . . you're wasting your time.

Vince Well, he killed himself, didn't he? No, but you would. I mean, if somebody found out, oh and in such a graphic way, oh and she does the whole scene for you, it's marvellous, she says, I came into the room, and I thought the room was empty. But it was not empty. It had two people in it and Stanley turn out that light and I thought she was marvellous in that scene but actually I do have to say that I didn't find that very uplifting, actually, and I said to myself then, I said, Vince, I said, you should stick to the musicals because you know that is more my thing really, well you know what I'm like, I'm sitting there, the orchestra's tuning up, the lights haven't even gone down yet and I'm off, oh no, I'm in a box at the opera, usually a bit younger is how I see myself in this scene, and very much in love, and there's nothing in the way, and I can just see myself travelling to all those far away places that I've always longed to visit, you know, Paris . . . Venice . . . or leaning against the rail of some ship gazing out at the stars and the sea, or standing on the beach of some tropical island with the palm trees sighing above us and then he puts his strong arms around me and then, suddenly, I'm back here pouring out a gin and tonic for some perfectly ordinary young man who has absolutely no idea what I'm thinking and why should he really, and I suddenly felt so utterly humiliated and defeated and so dreadfully, dreadfully ashamed, and I know you don't approve of women smoking in public and I don't either, really, but I had to have something to calm my nerves and I thought it might help.

Neil *lights* **Vince**'s *cigarette.*

Because, you see, I always have been the sensitive type.
So I expect I shall build up to it quite gradually. My boyfriend will leave me for someone younger and more attractive. Then I shall start to misbehave in public, raise my voice, wear scarves at parties, that sort of thing. Oh, yes, people will be able to tell what I'm thinking just by looking at me.
Drinking heavily does seem to be advised in most of the literature, so I've made a start on that one already as you can see.

Gin. And tonic, was it, sir?
Ice? Lemon? There you are then, sir, and that will only cost you one and six. (*He drinks the gin. Everyone breaks.*)

Neil Just remind me what year we're in here, Nicolas.

Nicolas It's 1958, I think, Neil.

Neil Oh, well, that's all right then. Nobody thinks like that any more.

Paul Certainly not.

Neil I mean, it's a very long time ago, isn't it?

Paul Get over yourself, that's what I say. Get modern, girl. I mean, if you were born in 1958 you'd be, well just work it out, you'd be –

Neil You'd be thirty-five.

Stephen And times change, don't they.

François Thank God . . . I mean, imagine, the West End in 1958, what was a queen like me supposed to do? Work as a waiter? Work as a 'speciality dancer' or end up stuck out here in the foyer selling programmes. Programmes, one shilling only. Programmes, one shilling only. (*Music.*)

Stephen Crew to the stage, please. Crew to the stage. And gentlemen of the chorus this is your fifteen minute call. Your fifteen minute call.

Music during which **Reg**, **Paul**, **Craig** *and* **François** *become the four Programme Sellers.*

François (*sings*)
Who's in the show,
The set, the plot, the frocks, the star.
Who's starting out and who'll go far –
You want to know –

Stephen, **Craig**, **Reg**, **Paul** (*sing*) Well, there you are

François Get your programmes here,

Craig containing full biographies for the whole company –

Stephen Telling you who is

Craig in the show

Paul and a full list of this evening's musical numbers, so that it all comes as no surprise, telling you who's who in which number and more importantly

François who isn't. Let's see what we have in store for you tonight . . . first of all, we have the Overture (*Music.*) which as you can hear is basically happy although it does hint (*Music.*) that things may get a little dramatic in the second half but then life's like that, then, Opening Chorus, 'Places, Please', Shaftesbury Avenue in the rain, all the lights on, meet the girl, see the show, it's just like real life, only . . . choreographed. Then – 'There You Are' duet (*Music.*) which as you can hear is the Boy Meets Girl scene, and then you have the Comedy Boy Meets Comedy Girl, 'You're Just The Ticket For Me' (*Music.*) which as you can hear is the same scene, only in 4/4 time, a little bit shorter and brighter –

Craig and they're a little bit shorter . . . and brighter.

Paul The Boy Meets Girl scene is where all the married couples in the audience have the opportunity to tenderly recall the scenes of their courtship, and the Comedy Boy Meets Comedy Girl, well, I think it's a very encouraging little scene, because it shows you how this sort of thing can happen even to people like you. Oh, I'm sorry, not to people like you. Like . . . the couple sitting just behind you.

François Which is what this show is all about really. Then you have the 'Love Is Never Easy' sequence

Neil First of all 'Not For Us', duet . . .
'Now Is The Time', duet –
'Not For Us', reprise.

Reg Oh, that sounds familiar. Now is the time but not for us –

François – then straight into the Act One Finale, full costume change. There will be one interval of fifteen minutes.

Paul There will, actually. Be an interval of fifteen minutes. (*Music: Intro.*) Bit of a chance to talk about how you think it's going (*They all pantomime an interval crowd.*) – a chance to, you know –

Reg Good evening, sir – are you two together? Oh, you are.

Craig If there's anyone you've spotted when they went in, now's your chance to . . .

François Here in London, it's never easy, is it, and it is the 1950s after all, but still . . . you manage . . .

Music: 'When Two People Meet'.

(*Sings.*) Eyes meet across a noisy room, a crowded bar – a
street – who knows . . .

Some people meet and not a word is said, he turns his head – one
    look – it shows . . .
I met him just like that and nobody saw
They were all there but no one knew
Some times it happens that . . . two people meet
And then you know, yes
Even then you know:
Tonight it could be – you . . .
                              Who knows
Sometimes there are no words that need be said –
We smiled instead, exchanged hellos
Though we had never met or spoken before
When he smiled all at once I knew.
That's how it happens when . . . two people meet
And so you know –
Yes, even then you know
Tonight it could be you.

Fifteen minutes. Don't waste them . . . and then Act Two, chorus,
full company, lots of Welcome Back acting, then off, and they carry
on with the plot:

Craig Trio, where they promise you everything is going to be all
right.

Reg Solo, where he says 'Gee, I hope everything is going to be all
right . . .'

Paul And then everything's all right, you get your production
number

François which tonight is set in the Wild West. And on Broadway.
And on a tropical island. Paris, of course, and Vienna. So I'm sure
that somewhere in the number we'll be able to take you to wherever
you want to go and I'm sure that somewhere all the boys will take
their shirts off and really jump which will be lovely and especially
for you, sir, but don't worry, nobody thinks that's what life is like
really. Nobody thinks that is what this show is really about and
then

Neil and then, either he has gone, and she comes downstage and
says, you know . . . I'm going to love him for ever, or he comes

back, and there's that bit where she comes downstage and says, you know I'm going to love him for ever, either way, people do really love each other, and that's what matters, that is what this show is all about.

Stephen That is what this show is about

François yeah, well, and then, 'The Same, Later That Evening' (*Music.*) which reminds us what life is actually like, but then you will be relieved to hear we move swiftly on to The Ballet (*Music.*) A lot of harps, as you can hear. The Ballet in this production is entitled 'There's Nothing In The Way' and the setting is, well, they fly all the scenery, I love it when they do that . . . this is the scene in the show where we get to see how life should be, or how it could be, and of course, it's all just a dream, but I promise you that when you see this number you will be in heaven, what I mean is, this is the one scene in the show which is like real life, it's just that it's real life in the future. And then you get the big dramatic ballad of the evening, entitled in this production:

Stephen 'Try Not To Be Too Unhappy: Just Remember That What Life Will Be Like Thirty-Five Years From Now Is Partly Your Responsibility'.

François And then, well, I'm sure you know how it ends . . . the lights all go down . . . and whatever had to happen has happened . . .

Paul I love this scene.

Craig I love watching it.

François You can hear the sound of his voice –

Reg (*to a gay man in the audience*) You'll love it. You can be anyone you want in this scene.

Stephen You could be her.

Reg You could be him. And we stand at the back and listen to the music.

François And he puts his strong arms around her – some of you may of course think that she is just imagining this happening – and then there's that bit where he says –

Music.

Neil You'd think we'd know better. Because he's not singing to me, is he? And it isn't you he's got his arms around. And those boys who stand around at the back when the lights go down, well they have to, because it's not their number. It couldn't be. It couldn't possibly be. And you know, it never is.

Neil, **François** And then

François you get your Finale. (*To music.*)

Reg And that'll be one shilling, thank you, sir. There you are.

Trevor Thank you . . . I can just see it . . .
These shows are all the same aren't they?
Oh, yes, here we are, 'Life Could Be Wonderful, duet'

Craig, **Trevor** (*sing*)
    Still when you're with somebody

Craig
    It's not just another show

François
    Nothing's gonna go wrong:

Francois, **Craig**
    Ev'ry song is your song!

François, **Craig**, **Trevor** How do I know? –

Trevor Well, like I said, some things you just know. (*Music ends.*)

Stephen This is your five minute call, gentlemen of the chorus, your five minute call. (**Stephen**, **François**, **Craig**, **Paul**, **Reg** *become ticket-tearers.*) So, if you could have your tickets ready please, ladies and gentlemen. If you could have your tickets ready please? If you could have your tickets ready please.

François If you could have your tickets ready please.

Paul Ten past ten, sir.

Reg Second aisle on the left.

Craig Down the stairs and to your right, madam.

François Actually, the programmes were on sale in the foyer, madam.

Stephen If you could have your tickets ready please. If you could have your tickets ready please. If you could have your tickets ready please. Thank you. Are you two together? Are you? Oh, I'm sorry, you're sitting in the balcony, if you could just leave the theatre, turn left and left again somebody might show you to your seats. If you could have your tickets ready please. If you could have your tickets ready please. If you could, that would make things a lot easier –
Because quite frankly, life can get a little difficult at this stage in the evening.
And I would just like to say that actually I find this sort of thing quite objectionable. And actually, this is exactly the sort of thing that I find offensive. And I would just like to say that personally, I agree with Mr John Osborne.
Does anyone happen to have a copy of the works of Mr John Osborne on their person?

Paul Yes, I do, actually. Well you never know, do you?

Stephen Mr John Osborne, ladies and gentlemen – and just remind me of the title of this particular work –

Boys *Look Back In Anger*.

Stephen And what a lovely title that is, ladies and gentlemen, *Look Back In Anger* – performed just after the year of my birth; and now that is what I call a proper piece of theatre, ladies and gentlemen. It's in black and white, lots of ironing and absolutely no musical numbers. And I quote.

Look Back In Anger page 36. 'I don't care which way he likes his meat. He's like a man with a strawberry birthmark; he insists on thrusting it in your face.'

Thank you very much John and I couldn't have put it better myself.
Because, let us be quite frank, ladies and gentlemen, we all know that there are a lot working in the theatre.

Vince A lot! Well, quite frankly I sometimes think if the ladies and

gentlemen actually knew what was going on at the back of the dress
circle during that number with the –

Stephen And I dare say there always will be. But do we need to
talk about it? I think not.
Because it's not as if they're actually running the building, is it? Is it?

Neil Well? Well quite. Because if that was the case I'm quite sure
the ladies and gentlemen would not feel quite so comfortable about
coming here after dark as they evidently do. I mean, imagine if you
were out on the town, if you were a man like my father – and this is
the 1950s, remember, and you went into . . . where, Reg?

Reg The Stockpot.

Neil and he takes a seat, and there are a group of men all wearing
make-up, raising their voices, not caring what people will say –
well, it would be upsetting, but at least he'd know that he could
complain to the management – and then imagine that later that
night a man like my father or a man like – well, like you, sir – good
evening, madam, goes to the theatre, and he takes his seat, the
curtain rises, and there is a group of men, wearing make-up, raising
their voices, singing,

Stephen 'Let people say we're – '

Neil We're in a very difficult situation. Here, on stage, we have, as
advertised, the classical post war musical narrative, boy meets girl,
and yet out there in the auditorium I cannot help but notice, for
instance, the couple sitting right behind you madam; or, to look at
the problem another way round, out there in the darkened
auditorium we do have, I am quite sure, several examples of the
classical post war musical narrative, boy meets girl, and yet up here
on stage the whole proceedings are, quite frankly, musical. And it
must be nearly 7.30 by now. The show is about to begin, the curtain
is about to rise, and, well, where are you?

*Music: 'There You Are': **Neil** and the **Boys**.*

Neil
   The one who sold your ticket
   The one who poured your drink
   The one who stood there smiling –

Reg
> Well, he's not what you might think

François
> The smart one selling programmes

Craig
> That will be one shilling, ta –

Craig, **Paul**
> Those two who stood behind you

Paul
> While you waited at the bar

Stephen, **Paul**, **Craig**
> Those three who seem to, well, stand out

Stephen, **Paul**, **Craig**, **Reg**
> Those four who we're not sure about –

François, **Neil**
> Look surely that's a bit too far –

All
> And what about you –

Neil
> Well
> There (**Neil** *indicating* **Boys**.)
> You (**Neil** *indicating audience*.)
> Are!!

All
> Of course there is a point of view
> That says of course there are a few
> But frankly that is nothing new
> And anyway we always knew
> And then just like you always do
> You take your places two by two
> The big surprise is
> When the curtain rises
> We're up here dressed up as YOU.

Stephen You must take your seats now, ladies and gentlemen.

Vince If I could ask you to drink up now please sir.

Reg Up the stairs and second aisle on the right, madam.

François Programmes. Programmes. Programmes.

Bells ringing during all this.

Bells end. One beat pause.

Stephen Front of house clearance: stand by everybody.

Vince Oh, it's such a relief when you've got the last one in.

Everyone quickly and quietly tidies up. **Trevor** *is standing like a lemon in the middle of the foyer getting in people's way. As they pass him*

Reg Oh, God, there's always one.
I hear music, but she isn't here . . .

Stephen I'm afraid I will have to ask you to take your seat now sir.

The stage is now clear except for **Vince** *and* **Trevor**.

Vince (*sings*)
    You wonder why you're waiting,
    Waiting to meet someone,
    Wondrin'

. . . where the fuck has she got to then.
Didn't she turn up then?
And about that drink for the interval, sir.
Just the one, will it be?

Tense pause: confrontation **Trevor/Vince**.

Seven chords. Exit **Vince**.

Music over which:

Trevor Waiting.
She was probably held up at work. Or by the rain – yes, that was probably it. I'm sure I told her what time it started –
Still, if we miss the opening number it's all there in the programme, I expect they'll end up together one way or another, don't you?
And if we do miss the opening number there's always a reprise. You know, that bit where they say they really love each other –

Well, hell, that's what matters –
That's what matters. The lights go down, he puts his arms around her, they've got their whole lives ahead of them, just like in all of these shows, and you know – well you know how it's gonna be, you can just see it, that's what life is like, you meet a girl, you buy her dinner, you take her to a show, you've found what you were waiting for, you know what happens next –

Beverley (*offstage microphone*) Nobody knows what's going to happen tonight. And it ain't so much a question of not knowing – something's coming, something – who knows
Maybe tonight
So hold my hand
And I'll take you there

Music ends. Long final bell.

Offstage mikes, as the Band enter and take their seats.

Paul I really must ask you to take your seat now, sir –

Reg Straight to the top of the stairs now, sir

François The show is about to begin

Stephen If I could hurry you along now, sir –

Nicolas Yes, sir, I will keep her ticket for her at the box office.

Craig Second aisle on the left, sir. Mind how you go –

Beverley, **Nicolas** Mind how you go in the dark.

Blackout complete, **Trevor** *takes his seat in the auditorium. Transformation music, complete Band.*

In the darkness, a dimly lit figure becomes visible: red-haired, smoking, back turned. Behind her, men in mackintoshes with umbrellas, frozen in tableau. It is **Beverley**, *the working actress, all dressed up for a 1950s night on the town. Coloured lights snap on.*

Beverley I love it when all the lights go down, don't you? That moment of . . . waiting for everything to start . . .

Music: 'Places Please'.

By six thirty it's getting dark –
The traffic's heavy round the Park

In Piccadilly and Leicester Square –
And of course on the Avenue where
On rainy nights
You see the lights
Reflected in the wet umbrellas
Held for eager girls by nervous fellas
Whose pace now quickens
As the traffic thickens
Buses! Newsboys! Folks arriving
Collars turned up – pavements shining –
People dashing –
Almost crashing –
Taxis splashing – they're setting you down
All dressed up for a night on the town

Craig, Stephen

But you don't care, 'cause it's exciting –
Now you're there – it's so inviting –

Beverley

All the sights and sounds to make your
Special night special are here so take your
Places Please, we're gonna give you a show
Places Please, that's what you came for we know
Who cares if outside it is raining
Come inside, where it is entertaining
Shows like these – no wonder ev'ryone goes –
Wait and see – soon you'll be tapping your toes – so –
You've got dreams that you know could come true
This is just the right show to come to –
Places Please, we're gonna give you a
Places Please, we're gonna give you a –
Show –
People never come late; on cue
At seven o'clock, they're arriving too –
Stage-door gossip in the corridor –
Swappin' all the stories from the night before
About those Boys –

And hear that noise –
As the band tunes up, all mixed with the din
Offstage hands flying that scenery in
Electricians
And technicians –
'Good house?' 'Not bad' – see the faces
Of the kids upstairs who got the best places –
Seven ten –
'House full' – then
Seven fifteen, 'Please hurry along now'
Seven twenty, ''Cause it won't be long now' –

All

Twenty-five – Off we go – Places Please – they're expectin' a –

*Dance break. Having shown us punters arriving, chorus boys arriving,
technicians preparing, the number now takes us into the dressing rooms:
powder puffs, costume changes, arguments over frocks, warm-up routines.*

Boys

Take your Places Please
Take your Places Please
Places Please! We can't wait sir
Places Please? Don't hesitate sir
Places – he's in a state
Places – she's never late
Places – we just can't wait!!!
Places Please
Six, seven and eight and

Beverley *and the* **Boys** *swing into full-blown opening number, dancing:
top hats, gloves, a spangled frock, high kicks.*

Ensemble

Places Please, we're gonna give you a show!
Places Please, 'cause what y've come for – we know
Something you can take your date to –
Don't you worry, so your girl is late? – you
Know that she's the kinda lady who'll show –

When she sees it she'll be telling you oh, oh, oh, oh!
You know that she loves you so, sir
It's show time, so off we go sir
Places Please, we're gonna give you a –
Places Please, we're gonna give you a –

At the top of the number, everything freezes. The lights turn blue. **Beverley**
sends her follow spot out into the auditorium, it hunts for **Trevor** *and finds*
him.

Beverley . . . you know, the first time I saw you, I thought, good
heavens . . . It can't be.
It can't possibly be. You look just like . . . I walked on, and, well,
everybody thinks musicals are about somebody else, don't they, but
tonight, I thought well, let's make tonight a special occasion, so:

Beverley *and the* **Boys** *sing simultaneously.*

Ensemble
Places Please   Places Please

Beverley
The lights go down   They always do

Ensemble
Places Please – Let's face it he's

Beverley
What does that curtain hide from view?

Ensemble
The nat'ral choice, he's

Beverley
The big surprise is

Ensemble
Got the voice, he's

Beverley
When it rises

Ensemble
Got the part; yes sir, it's YOU – Yeah!

Beverley

That tonight the show is YOU – Yeah!

The follow spot has pulled **Trevor** *onto the stage; he finds himself caught, centre stage, framed by the company in the Act One curtain tableau.*

Interval.

Act Two

Music: reprise Act One ending. Very loud and strange as curtain goes up; company in exact repeat of end of Act One as if they had been holding it all this time.

Seven chords: everyone is waiting. Seven chords again: they all look at **Trevor**. *He clearly doesn't know what's going on.*

Violin phrase. The **Boys** *take a very conspicuous break – as if an understudy rehearsal with an understudy they don't like had been called – they go off into their corner to appear insolently unconcerned but in fact of course they are always ready to swoop into place at any moment.*

Craig Oh, fabulous. That's fabulous, that's all we need, how long have we been doing this show?

All Years.

Craig And I mean, years. Night after night after bleeding night.

François And now they send us a leading man who doesn't know what happens next.

Paul Treacherous, that's what I call it.

Reg Oh, give the kid a chance.

Stephen Thank you.

They continue to chatter quietly under the following:

Beverley (*to* **Trevor**) I love that moment when the lights go down, don't you? That feeling of . . . (*Seven chords.*) waiting. Sometimes it seems to go on for ever. (*She luxuriates in a phrase from the clarinet as time expands . . .*) Yes, and?

Trevor I was sitting in my seat and . . . you came on. And now I'm not sitting in my seat any more.

Beverley Well, and now what happens? (*No response from* **Trevor**.) Try looking in your programme.

Trevor I . . . I don't seem able to find it.

Beverley Oh, really. Let's see if we can remember. Opening number, Shaftesbury Avenue in the rain, full chorus, and then –

Trevor 'There You Are' – Boy Meets Girl, oh, my God – I'm terribly sorry –

Beverley That's right, she isn't here –
Don't worry. You left her ticket for her at the box office, remember. There's nothing you can do. And anyway I'm sure it's not 7.30 yet. Not quite. (**Beverley** *plays with the absence of his girl.*) And you can't really have A Show without A Girl, can you? (*Pause. Is she putting herself forward for the part?*) You know, sometimes I feel just before I go on, that tonight anything could happen, I mean, who knows – I could play anyone, who do I want to be tonight!!! – but you know, boys – you know, boys – you know, I could never be his girl. I couldn't be. I couldn't possibly be. Oh, you want to be her, you promise yourself that you could be, one day – or used to promise yourself that you would be . . . but . . . no, don't tell me, she's nice and steady, she's so, well usually she's so reliable. She's well-dressed – but not too well-dressed – it's her best suit – blue?

Trevor No, grey actually.

Beverley I can just see her, she looks just like – well of course, when I imagine her, she looks just like my mother.
And I'm glad for you, I really am – we're all glad for you; we heard your . . . news. Congratulations. You're very good at it you know – that's why we picked you. You're a natural – I loved all that watch business in the first act, you know, looking at it all the time so that no one would think you were . . . single.
(*To audience.*) It's so touching isn't it, the way he's trying to get it all right – and well, you've all seen a show before, you know something is bound to go wrong – it would be a little bit disappointing if it didn't.
(*To* **Trevor**.) So (*Pause.*) we'll just wait (*Pause.*) till she gets here. It's still not quite 7.30 – oh, my watch seems to have stopped.

Trevor So's mine.

Beverley Well, shows like this always end happily, don't they? (*As* *she exits.*) Let's just assume she's on her way. So, you're standing there, waiting, and then – Pick it up on the Act Two opening number boys, full chorus, two, three, four!!

*The **Boys** take their time deciding whether they are going to help this man out or not. Eventually they pounce; they disorientate him with a flurry of instructions.*

Reg So what have we got here? Right. Sit down, look in the mirror, tell yourself you are going to get through this, and remember the essentials. ONE . . . OK, come on girls.

Paul Sorry, we were sorting something out.

Reg I'll sort you out in a minute.

All ONE!

Reg They're looking at you. (*Pause.*) And that's all you need to know. And then you'll need the Tools of the Trade; I like to have them all laid out in a row before I start: Exhaustion

Stephen Exasperation

François Desperation

Craig Humiliation

Beverley Rejection

Paul A quick drink

Reg and a little Number 9 for the cheeks.

François Of course, it helps if you've got The Body –

Music.

Craig So that the very first time they see you they say

Craig, François My God . . .

Stephen The arms . . .

Paul The attitude

François The technique

Reg And most of all you've got to really look the part, which in your case means you have to look as though you're not playing a part at all . . . now, how can I put it . . .

Music: 'You Gotta Have Conviction'.

(*Sings.*) When you're just starting out you'll find
That knowing which step to take –
And knowing what Place is your proper place –
And showing the World that Make-
Up's not something you put on your face
But something you do with your mind . . .
Knowing just which way in Life to turn . . .
Isn't something you know . . . but . . . Learn!! So . . .
Remember that
It needs attack
E-spesh-ly when you're at the back –
Even when you
Make an exit –
Hit them when no one expects it!
Arm – Extend
And bend – don't frown –
And Lift the Chest – good, Shoulders Down.
And Lift the Chin
And Stomach in!
And – Chin! and AND! and ONE! – the HAND!
and TWO the Wrist
Yes, get the gist?
The BACK! – and THREE! Please watch that knee
AND FOUR – THE CHEST!
And one bar's rest –
    JUST FOLLOW ME!!

Keep it light
Tight
Now twice as Bright and Twice as quick – Again!

Boys
You gotta have Conviction –

Reg
'Cause it looks
Right
AND LEFT and travel travel KICK! AND when

Boys

It's done with conviction

Reg

The trouble that you took
To look better than you look
May seem, well, a little forced at first –
It may somehow seem 'not real',
Feeling better than you feel –
But Art, like Life, believe me's best – Rehearsed!
So:
Give it Height!
Bite!
And then despite the role – FACE UP!

Boys

You gotta have conviction:

Reg

Even quite
Trite
Routines can light the whole place up

Boys

If done with conviction –

Reg

If it looks as though we're lying
Look again, in fact, we're trying
Nothing quite like Pace to quell a doubt
If you've got a number, sell it (you bet)
If you know the story, tell it (oh, very Grace Kelly)
If you don't, oh well, still spell it out –
'Cause it's not
Plot
But what you've got that makes a great show!

All

Yes, sir, we've got conviction

Reg

Yes, I'm sure

Your
Material is second rate – so what!
'Cause if you've got conviction
You're never at a loss

Stephen
As you boldly step across

François
That fine old line of distinction

Paul
That separates the act

Craig
Of a talented Young Fact

Reg
From the creaking of a Tired Old Fiction – Ah-Ha!

Stephen, **François**, **Paul**, **Craig**
Which goes to show
It's really true:
S'not WHAT you do, but HOW you do:

Reg (*speaks*) Try and stay with me on this one, Nicolas. Please.
The only thing that really proves
If he has got it's how he moves.

Nicolas Two, three, four.

All (*sing*)
The only thing that really proves
If he has got it's how he moves.

The number ends in a tableau; applause button/hold pose/brief music reprise, regroup in final tableau. Hold. **Trevor** *is pretty hopeless, and in particular he doesn't smile in the tableau.*

Trevor Why are you smiling?
Severally:

Craig Because if you smile and grit your teeth at the same time . . . you can get your breath back.

François One has to relax somehow.

Paul And also because there's a certain sense of triumph at having got through that particular part of the evening. And you want to let them know that there's a lot more coming their way.

Trevor What are we looking at?

Beverley The future.
That's why you don't look directly at them. They all think you're looking straight into someone's eyes – but not theirs. Somebody else's. You have got to make everyone feel they're included –

Reg Especially the kids in the gallery.

Beverley But you don't want anybody thinking that the future is, you know, personal – so you try and hit the dress circle lights, which gives the impression you're looking out there into that bright new day on their behalf –

Craig and they look at you

Paul looking at it

Stephen and you're

All Smiling!

François So, what can you see?

Trevor I'm going to be a father.

Beverley Yes, good, and, Details. And Keep Smiling.

Trevor It's going to be . . . No, no, I can see it
It's going to be
It's going to be
Everything's going to be . . .

Stephen Trevor is very happy to be here tonight

Craig He is delighted to be appearing in a West End show

Stephen And what he wanted to say was, when you have been looking forward to something as long as he has been looking forward

Craig When you've been looking forward to – that special night out

Stephen When you've been waiting as long as we've been waiting, then – a show like this

François Shows like these

Craig Well –

François It could be just what you need

Reg Every single night! Except Sundays.

Craig And how long have we been doing it –

Stephen Years

Craig And I mean years

Reg . . . night after night . . .

Beverley Night After Night –

Reg (*taking a heavy volume from* **Beverley**) or . . . *A Complete History Of The Theatre.*
Date of birth? (**Reg** *looks for the right page.*)

Trevor I was born in 1928.

Reg 1928 . . . Hit show of 1928?
No, No, Nanette. Hit song of *No, No, Nanette?*
Not doing very well so far, are we? Two, three, four –

Boys 'I Want To Be Happy' –

Reg There you are, you see, completely predictable so far; you were born, you wanted to be happy . . .

Paul 'But I can't be happy'

Reg Thank you!
1934 *Anything Goes*
1935 *Glamorous Nights*
1936 *Careless Rapture* . . . ah well, it's what you do when you're a young man isn't it? –

Craig (*to* **Paul**) I don't remember him in that –

Reg (*to* **Trevor***, in 'Novello' style*) Do you remember? –

Trevor No, no, you see – I was born in '28.

Reg So? And how old do you think I am?

Stephen It doesn't matter what age you were. You can remember things you never saw, just like you can look forward to things you may never have. That's the thing about shows. About shows like those –

François Shows like these . . . moonlight – footlights; it may all seem very long ago, or very far away, but just remember . . . well

Reg When you remember –

Craig People say of course in those days, but, well it still gets dark every night. The moon still rises

Music: 'Those West End Nights'.

Craig, François
    Each night the hour must come again
    When day fades to a dream
    When cares must cede to joy
    When siren voices call
    As shadows fall –
    Each night, the spell is cast again –
    Those lights – that first applause –
    Those first sweet notes of melody –
    And then . . . the night is yours . . .
    Once more, a stage-door rendezvous
    Once more a Promise made
    Once more, a West End night
    Those painted stars above
    Those songs of love . . .
    Once more, the thrills that must be had
    The tears that must be wept
    Each night, the chance of happiness
    Each night, the promise kept . . .

During this song, the **Boys** *conjure an image of the pre-war West End: moonlight, star-cloth, show-boys striking poses, a dancer in harem pants and jewels. The vision disappears with the final notes of the song.*

Paul I know how you feel. I feel the same sometimes, and I'm in it. I mean it's not much use to you when you're back in your flat thinking about the morning. People say to me, I don't know how you can, I mean it's all just a big dream sequence, isn't it really, all those, you know, colours, and I say –

Reg Don't say it, dear, you'll only upset yourself. Oh, go on then, say it.

Paul I say yes, but you can quite understand people wanting to go out in the evenings, I mean with the way things are, and then when you think about how they might be, well by the end of an average day you do quite often feel like just bursting into . . . song.

Music: 'Set Your Life To Music'. **Paul** *sings while tap dancing.*

> You've got to have hope
> No matter what life's bringing.
> You've got to have hope
> That's easy when you're singing.
> If your life's like mine and gets you down
> If you find you just can't cope
> You just set your life to music
> These days
> You've got to have hope.
> Look what life is bringing.
> Still you keep on singing.
> These days ev'rybody's got to have Hope. (*Music ends.*)

Go on, try again.

Trevor It's going to be a boy. I'm going to have a son. Tell me what he's going to look like. How's he going to move, what's he going to do for a living – and how is any of this going to happen if she doesn't turn up. I mean, you can't have a show without a girl, can you?

Beverley Oh, come on, give the kid a chance.
Now, where were we?

Trevor I was sixteen when the war ended.

Craig 1945: *Perchance To Dream*

Trevor Then, of course, I did my National Service, well it's what you do when you're a young man, isn't it?

Craig 1947: *Annie Get Your Gun*

Trevor We met in '51.

Craig 1951: *Oklahoma . . . South Pacific*

Stephen '. . . You May Meet A Stranger' – upstairs in the crush bar of the Royal Opera House, in the second interval of *Norma*, and when you have met him, you feel –

Craig you feel – *The King And I* – 1953

Trevor We were married in 1954.

Craig 1954: *Bells Are Ringing*
1955: *The Pyjama Game*

Paul, **Craig**, **Stephen** 1957: Judy Garland at the London Palladium

Stephen 'I Could Go On Singing . . .'

Reg And so there you are. The story of your life. You wanted to be happy, perchance to dream; you were doing what came naturally. It was an enchanted evening, you could have danced all night, people did say you were in love, bells were ringing and now tonight, tonight –

Trevor Tonight –

Reg 1958 – *West Side Story* – something's coming, something good, so I really don't see what you've got to worry about –

Beverley *sees that* **Reg** *has gone one page too far.*

Oh, *West Side Story*, that was the show for me. Did you see it? I was right upstairs in the gods, and when that curtain went up

Paul Well, it's silly looking back really, but it was the 1950s you see, and those dancers, well we'd never seen anything like it

Reg and I looked down on that stage and I just thought, that's it. That's where I want to be. (*Cuts himself off.*)
And then at the end, I don't know if you remember it, they've got their whole lives ahead of them, they've arranged to meet that evening, and then he gets a message to say she isn't coming, he's never going to see her again, ever, and he can't believe it, he just can't believe that's what happens, and then he's standing there, for a moment there's no music, and suddenly he thinks he hears the sound of her voice and he turns and –

Beverley What night did *West Side Story* open?

Stephen December 12th, 1958. Her Majesty's Theatre. I knew the stage manager.

Trevor So what night is this?

Beverley Exactly, what night is this? Anybody got a programme?

Craig One rainy night, early spring of 1958 –

Reg – so he should be born in about –

Trevor When? When's he going to be born. Tell me!

Boys' *reaction: refusing to tell him.*

Beverley Good! Sounds like we'd better carry on with the plot.

Reg TRIO!! Where they promise you –

François – everything is going to be all right you know.

Reg SOLO – Where he says, Gee

Trevor I hope so.

Beverley Dress circle lights, remember.

Trevor Yes, that's fine when you're out there, they make everything clearer – but when you're up here, they make it harder. To see. What's going to happen.

Beverley You've got your whole life ahead of you.

Trevor Yes, but how do you know what's actually going to happen?

Beverley Do you need to?

Trevor Oh, yes, you go out for the evening, you want a good story. Everybody needs to know . . . who you're playing.

Beverley You did OK so far, didn't you? Listen, let me tell you something: worried about your part? Worried what lies ahead? Worried things might get a little tricky in the second act? Well, believe me, darling, we know exactly how you feel – but remember, tonight is a special occasion . . . when the lights go down and that curtain rises

François We can take you wherever you want to go –

Beverley You can be anyone you want. Jump in!!

François The clothes are always so much better in the past, don't you think, you walk on, and when people see you they think – Fabulous . . .

Stephen And if it's in the past then when we get to that scene, you know, where they hold hands and they say Gee, I wonder what is going to happen – ?

Craig Well, it's touching really, because we'll already know, won't we?

Beverley We'll be looking back at them looking forward – just like I expect you're looking forward to looking back at tonight.

Paul You know where you are with the past, don't you?

Reg So . . . where are we tonight?

Trevor Well, tonight, tonight we're right here.

Music: 'Anywhere But Here'.

François (*sings*)
    When you go out of an evenin', you want that sense of . . . well, of leavin',
    Of travellin' to some place you've never been –

Stephen
    Without leaving your seat . . .

Craig, **Reg**
    Without moving your feet

Boys
    We will take you to some unfamiliar scene. (*Exit* **Boys** *to change.*)

Beverley
    A different way of walking
    A different way of talking –
    Sometimes in life there's nothing like a change
    And though things may seem strange, they're clear
    You somehow seem to know that we're
    Not anywhere
    But somewhere
    That's anywhere but

Enter **Boys**, *dressed as technicolour farm-hands: neckties, waistcoats, hats, bales of straw, etc.*

Beverley, **Stephen**, **Craig** Here.

Exit **Beverley** *to change.*

Boys
> Where there's corn ripe for reapin' and fences for leapin'
> There's dawgs and there's hawgs and there's steers –

Craig, **Stephen**
> Such wide open spaces and wise friendly faces and skies oh
> So high and so clear –

François
> And your girl's just been bakin'
> A pie that she's takin'
> In her clean white aprin'

Enter **Beverley**, *dressed in De Mille gingham and petticoats.*

> Gee we're

Boys
> So darned glad we're not anywhere –
> Who could live anywhere –
> Who would be anywhere but here!

Hoe down dance break. Yee-hah etc. Each dance break involves **Beverley** *being passed around and ending up with* **Trevor**. *She is the wrong girl for him. Exit* **Boys**.

Beverley If that wasn't what you paid for
We can always change the décor . . .
And it's not like life, all grey and insecure (*Sings:*)

> Ev'ry detail lets you see
> There's no finer place to be
> 'Cause we're somewhere that's
> Somewhere!
> Try anywhere –
> Like here!

Exit **Beverley**, *enter* **Boys**, *dressed as technicolour sailors.*

Boys
> Where?

Reg
> Here!

Boys
On some lousy beach with the goils kept outta reach
Feeling horny and so far away from home
And well when you're feeling lonesome
Your mind it starts to roam some
Till you're smarting up your hair with brush and comb

Stephen
You got palm trees and a sunset –

Paul
Those native girls are fun – yet

Reg
Still you wish you could be dockin' at a pier

Stephen
And puttin' your best whites on

Craig
Seein' Broadway with its lights on
All dressed up for a date in your best gear . . .

Enter **Beverley**, *dressed as a South Pacific girl – GI shorts, lei.*

All
Then you'd say

Trevor
Hey, where to babe?

Reg
She'd say

Beverley
Well, that's up to you babe . . . Anywhere – like anywhere!! –
just gemme outta here!

Swift danced exit: sailors on the town with their girls. **Stephen** *remains, changes on stage.*

Stephen Farmers, cowboys, gigolos,
We've played them; gangsters, matelots –
Just say the word and (click) we will appear. (*Sings:*)

We can change the whole location
Just by changing occupation
'Cause we're anything –
Wear anything –
Want anything? We're (*Exit* **Stephen**.)

Reg (*dressed as a maitre d'*) Here . . . we are, sir. Dining . . . alone, sir? Still, let's try and make tonight a – special occasion. Ah, sir – (*Sings:*)

Do you recall – those happy days – of oysters served on silver
    trays
Gypsy bands, Lily Elsie in sable – caviar – at your usual table –
The linen

Enter the **Boys** *dressed as waiters with trays of champagne.*

The crystal – the vast polished floor –
Well just for tonight boys, let's do it once more.
(*Spoken.*) Here she comes! Here she comes! She makes her

Enter **Beverley** *dressed in full high Edwardian finery, bustle and feathers.*

Beverley
She makes her entrance late again
Things look great again
Celebrations start here;
They're so good to me –
So they should be –
We've been together for years – good evening Gaston –
You can watch them
But you can't touch them
They feel safe when I'm near
'Cause this is the place where every single one
Yes everyone
Yes! Everyone is –

Beverley *plus* **Boys**
Working late again!
Looking great again
Lights grow bright when she's near
Violins again

Beverley	**Boys**
Double gins again	
Yes sir	Bless her!
Oh yes sir	Oh yes sir
She's here!!	She's here!

Beverley (*changing on stage into Montmartre chanteuse. Spoken*)
Of course a change of setting
May not change what you're getting
For some people, the story stays the same (*Music goes French.*)
You are looking for . . . your girl, non?

Enter **Stephen** *and* **Craig** *as* les mecs, *rivals for* **Beverley**'s *affections.*
They beat **Beverley** *up for talking to a stranger. They beat each other up.*
The Apache. One of them gets knifed. Tableau.

Tableau hidden by screens by **Paul**.

Paul (*while changing. Spoken*)
You need to know just where you are
And when you do, well – there you are!
All you need now's a partner –

Trevor Yes I know

Paul
A different style of costume
Ev'ry time. Do we get lost – you might well ask:
The answer is, of course, well, no

Boys (*sing*)
Because we've made a whole career
Out of re-al-ising we're

Paul Not really here

Boys
Not anywhere
Not anywhere
Not anywhere
But . . .

The **Boys** *and* **Trevor** *dress themselves as cadets or officers from an*
operetta: epaulettes, braid, white gloves, silver and blue.

Craig
  . . . hear
The orchestra playing
It's easy! your body starts swaying . . .
When that melody sings from the score
There in your arms is the one you adore
Then you turn on the beat and
Sweep her right off her feet and
Then you know as you're taking the floor
That we are not here now – not any more –
Then it all becomes clear
What you wanted my dear
You wanted to be
What you couldn't be . . . anywhere
Anywhere
But here!

Enter **Beverley** *in stage-filling white ostrich-trimmed Jeanette Macdonald crinoline.*

Boys
  Anywhere, but anywhere, but anywhere, we're everywhere, yes
     everywhere, we're everywhere

Beverley Yes, everybody gets to be just who they've always wanted to be. Just look at them. No wonder they love getting paid to do it. And what about me? Did you like me? Did you like me like that?

  (*Sings.*) Tell me how you'd like me – would you like me like this?
  If I played a girl like this, would I be the kind you'd kiss
  Would I be the kind you'd want to, well, romance with?
  Everybody needs a girl to dance with
  So!

Beverley	**Boys**
Tell me how you'd like me	
Would you like me like this	Could you like me like this
Tell me how you'd like me	
Should you like me like this	Should you like me like this
	If I played a man like this
Really not the kind you'd kiss	

Really not the kind you'd want	Then I'd be the kind I'd want
To well romance with	want To well, romance with
	Look it's really up to you
What you want, I can do	Everybody needs a girl to –
Well, to dance with	Well, to dance with

Ensemble

Tell me how you'd like me
Go on, just say it
Anyway you'd like me
I've done it, can play it
Just tell me how you want me

Beverley	**Boys**
Just say it my dear	Just make sure that we're
Just anyone	
Well anyhow	
Anyway	Just anywhere
Anyway	Anywhere
I'm here	Anywhere
	But here!

The number ends with all the **Boys** *dragging up in an aggressively sexual parody of the previous costume changes; all the costumes of the number worn by the wrong people in the wrong way. Triumphant exit, leaving* **Beverley** *collapsed in a full curtsey.*

Beverley It's not easy you know. Darling, could you – no? No, well, just help yourself to a drink while I'm changing. (**Beverley** *changes onstage.*)
Every night before I come on at the end of the first act I have that line, nobody knows what is going to happen tonight, and I always tell myself, right, tonight, tonight, who do I want to be tonight, after all none of you know what I'm like in real life, I could play it any way I want to, and all the time I'm thinking, darling, I know what happens, I know what they want, that's the whole point, that's what I get paid for – (*She is now in a little white dress.*) That's better, isn't it? 'Cause you didn't like me like that did you, I know, I know, well, it isn't easy and nobody said it would be. It's a tough part, but – congratulations – somebody had to play it.

Trevor I suppose it had to be me.

Beverley Oh yes. It had to be you. Because how is it going to be, we want to know. How is it going to be when he grows up? Is it going to be all right?

Trevor It has to be.

Beverley Exactly. It has to be. That's why you came tonight. That's why they came. That's why I came, that's why I'm in this dress, and – that's why the music now changes . . . and why she has to be sorry she shouted at you in that last number, because, well because there is always a scene where things go wrong, where somebody doesn't turn up. Somebody's waiting. Somebody's scared. Somebody's heart is breaking, minute by minute. Well, this is it. (**Boys** *enter. Music.*)
The lights go down, the boys stand around at the back, and she's – you know how she feels, don't you? This is the scene where she says look I really don't know how I can go on with this any more.

Stephen But then one of the boys comes on and he sees her standing there, and he knows how she feels, so he says it's a beautiful night, because . . . because he wants her to sing. You don't want to be her, really, do you? It's all right that it isn't your scene, because she knows how you feel. How you feel when you're waiting for that special someone. She knows that's what matters. That is what matters. (*Music: 'Life Could Be Wonderful'.*)
And so he says, are you OK?

Beverley And she says, oh, sure, I'll just sit here for a while. And yes, the lights have gone down, and yes the boys are standing quietly at the back, and yes, she knows how much they need this. And she can see you, watching her, and she knows – (*To the audience.*) this is how you feel, this is how it feels when you're on your own. On your own, in the dark, and . . . thinking about . . . him. (*Sings.*)

They always told her one day life could be wonderful
One shining moment when her life would be wonderful
You'd think she'd know by now, have heard it all before
Have heard too many songs to believe them any more
Each time I play this scene I tell myself it's not me – but then
Each night I play this scene so well I think maybe again

Tonight it could be true
If it was, then that would be wonderful – for you.

They always told her he'd come back one day, wonderful
You'd think I'd know by now, you'd think I wouldn't cry –
We know that lovers dream, we know that lovers die –
She tells herself that any moment now he will be there
She'll close her eyes she'll hold her breath she'll turn and touch
    his hair
Tonight it must be true
If it's not, then
That would be – (*Music break.*)

Craig *appears in a white Émile de Becque dinner jacket.*

Craig
I thought you'd know by now
I thought you'd know for sure
I thought a heart could tell when it's alone no more
Tonight I'm here and now I'm here I swear I'll never leave

Beverley
How will you know?

Craig
Tonight I'll take you in my arms and I'll make you believe

Beverley
How will you know – know that you still believe

Craig, **Beverley**
Tonight it's all come true, now life will be wonderful with you.

Neil They always promise you that, 'one day', one day you'll have
it all.

Reg You, not someone else, you. All of you. All kinds of people.

Craig And every night when I hear that line I tell myself, well,
that's not long to wait, is it? I'll just wait.

Stephen I'll just have to wait.

François I'll just have to wait.

Paul I'll wait.

Reprise of tableau: 'Looking Into The Future'. Seven chords. Suddenly
Trevor *leaps up as if he was getting up from his seat, squeezing past the rest of the people in a row of theatre seats in a panic to get out.*

Trevor Excuse me, excuse me, I've got to go and – did anybody see her? Maybe she went to the wrong theatre, or – Oh NO! (*Music.*)

Beverley Later that same evening – of course, some of you may think he's just imagining this happening.

François Maybe he didn't get her message.

Craig I knew there'd been an accident, the rain's been terrible tonight.

Reg Oh that's awful.

Stephen You know she's pregnant –

Paul Oh, my God.

Trevor *bursts through the crowd of onlookers: she isn't there. Tableau.*

François It has to happen to somebody. (*Music ends.*)

Stephen It isn't anybody's fault – and of course when you're just listening to the songs you don't remember what actually happens in the story, do you?

Reg It was on the television one afternoon last week, I hadn't seen it in years, I'd completely forgotten that scene. You know that scene where – look, everybody knows that musicals aren't about someone else, they're about people just like us really.

Paul People just like you, and like the couple sitting behind you.

Reg But not that scene. I mean it happened. It had to happen but not to . . . that's not me, that's not me with that look on my face.

Beverley And then there is always someone who says: 'Who knows what could happen?'
'All kinds of things happen.'
'You got to keep on caring what's going to happen – '

Trevor You tell me why I feel like this. Why should I be scared? Of course, when you're listening to the song you get scared that you could lose – that she'll lose him – but look, you know they'll end up together, they'll have the whole of their lives ahead of them. He always comes back to her in the end!

François Well, that's worse, isn't it?

Paul If you think someone's lost and then they come back, that's worse. Because you can't help thinking about the one you lost or who the person next to you lost and who never came back and who never will now. I always cry when I'm standing at the back there and God knows I've seen it enough times.

Some people waited and waited and then they found their special someone and it's all right now, everything's going to be all right now – but you know – you know, boys (*To the* **Boys** *in the audience.*), and you know (*To the whole audience.*) some people waited and waited and they never did. And I know you'll say everybody is waiting and that's right, I know that, but some people have to wait just a little bit longer and a little bit harder and then sometimes there aren't enough days and there aren't enough years. Everybody has got to think about the future but sometimes it isn't there. It doesn't start and that is why there is crying at this point in the show. If the music stopped, if the music were to ever stop, for just a moment and if we listened then we would hear it.

They're doing it as quietly as they can but the sound is still there. When you cry like that it's best to do it in the dark.

You do it for all the people who heard this song and saw him come back and who said it isn't me, it couldn't be. It's not for us, it never is, and you cry for the fact that there isn't anything you can do now to tell them otherwise. And even if you could promise me that there is going to be time, that there is going to be a time when people won't have to wait quite so hard or quite so long, that sound will still be there. I hired a tape from the video shop and we watched it together and when it got to this scene, you know, the big scene, the one just before the end, I swear I could hear the sound of people crying on the soundtrack, it was there on the actual tape. And I don't think it is ever going to go away, that sound, not ever.

We hear the voices of some of the people he has been talking about.

Stephen Are you two together? Are you

François Let's see what we have in store for you tonight . . .

Craig When you're with somebody, it's not just another show . . .

Reg Some people I know spend a great deal of their time waiting. And I mean years.

Regroup: 'Looking Into The Future' tableau.

Paul (*to* **Trevor**) You have got to think about the future, haven't you?

Music. **François**, **Craig** *wordless duet.*

Trevor Why am I going on like this? He ain't even been born yet . . . but I can see just exactly – but I can't

Beverley 'He'd better look a lot like me' . . .

Trevor 'The spittin' image' – I can't see it –

Beverley But you said –

Trevor Yes, I know, but I can't –

Beverley I think you'll find that if you look in your programme, sir –

Trevor I can't find it.

Beverley Try and remember what it said. Think. This is important!

Trevor What life will be like thirty-five years from now . . . This is the scene

Beverley This is the scene . . .

Trevor This is the scene

Beverley the scene which is just like real life, only it's real life in the future. This is the scene where we see how life could be. Thank you.

Music.

François Places please. Take him through it one last time –

Reg Chest. Face up. Shoulders down.

François OK, now we go into the Ballet.

Reg Remember – they're looking at you. You're not watching. You don't know –

François Say it again.

Trevor I don't know what's going to happen –

François OK.

Reg 1928. You were born and then, 1945, you're sixteen years old. You've got your whole life ahead of you.

François Let's see . . . there's nothing in the way . . .

Reg 1948, you're a young man, up in town. (*Music.*)
1952, you meet that special someone. (**Trevor** *embraces* **François**.)

Paul Do it as if you were scared you could lose them.
Do it as if you had never been allowed to hold someone like that.

Craig Do it as if you did it every day. As if you were used to being together.

François As if it was all just a dream.

Beverley And then –

Reg 1954, almost four years ago exactly, you got married. (*Wedding tableau with music.*)

Beverley And now –

Reg And now, one rainy night in the early spring of 1958. Tonight.

Beverley Tonight.

Stephen *appears dressed exactly as* **Trevor** *in hat and coat. He dances a dance of anxiety and expectation.*

The Ballet. **Trevor** *is dreaming his future. In the distance, like a mirage he sees a perambulator. But no, it really is there.*

Beverley She told you you were going to be a father. Remember.

Trevor *takes a step forward as if in his dream he wanted to reach the child. Storm clouds appear in the sky.*
*The black figures crowding around the pram scatter. It has gone. In its place is a vision of the man the child will become: Dancing Neil (***François***).*
Alone, unaware of being watched, Dancing Neil dances a dance of splendid youth. He is different to the other men who are dark and faceless, he jumps and plays and mocks them.
He meets his father, Dancing Trevor. **Trevor**, *still dreaming, sees himself meeting his own son. Adjustments, conflict, how are they to relate to each other,*

should they or could they embrace, is this all just a dream or are you really here? Pas de deux. They finally embrace. Final lift, father lifts son. Slow descent from lift; they separate; it was a dream. Music: 'No One Knows'.

Trevor . . . the dream that ev'ry other dad and mother dream . . . and when tonight is many years ago, I'll dream with you, and we'll be glad that our dream came true, and strange as it may seem, this song will echo in your dream – (**Neil**.) because you know what has to be said at the end of the evening.

Beverley You've got to have a dream

Neil Got to have a dream worth a keepin'.

Beverley If you don't have a dream (*Sings.*)

No one can say what the years hold in store
And no one can tell you, or so it seems.
Yet you hear all your hopes in the words of a song
You see them in the world of your dreams.
No one can know and nobody can show
You what lies ahead or why these dreams still fill your heart.
Though dreams can fade and songs deceive you know you must
    believe
That tonight the life you've longed for could start.
Hold on to Hope, hold on to your dreams

Neil, Stephen Places please   Take your places please.

Beverley
Hold on tight although you fear they be bro-ken
Those dreams are all you have tonight
Tonight they're all you need
What tomorrow brings . . . no one knows . . .

Craig, François
Tonight again they're waiting, they have seen so many shows
They've been waiting for so many nights
Tonight they're gonna see
How tomorrow's gonna be.

Neil and when they see me . . . when people see me
When people see me, they say, My God

Beverley It must be you. It has to be you.

Neil You look just like he did. I even move like he does. This is my father's body. My chest, chin and arms are like his. I hold my shoulders like he does. This is his hair. I can tell you in what year it will turn grey; I can show you where the lines on my face will be. His suits fit me. People do say to me all the time –

Beverley What time is it?

Music suspends.

Neil They say – you look just like your father's son.

Music indicates that time starts again. Everyone looks at their watches; then everyone suddenly looks up as if someone had arrived in the theatre. It is her at last. We hear the **Boys** *usher her to her seat.*

Craig Oh, yes, madam, he left your ticket for you at the box office.

François The Overture is just about to begin, madam.

Reg Stand by everybody.

Stephen If you'd come this way

Paul And if I could ask you to hurry along now please

Stephen Straight to the top of the stairs, madam.

François Second aisle on the left and –

Reg, **Craig** Mind how you go in the dark –

Neil And then she says, Oh, darling, I'm so sorry I'm late, and then there's that bit where he says, It doesn't matter, nothing matters, just so long as you're here

Beverley And then the lights are about to go down –

Reg Stand by house lights.

Neil And he puts his arm around her –

Beverley Go house lights.

Reg, **Beverley**, **Neil** Stand by curtain.

Neil They sit there in the dark and they hold hands.

All Good luck everybody.

The curtain is about to rise. The Overture (reprise) starts.

Neil What will be the changes, you never can imagine. He never could have imagined who these arms of mine would hold, what this body of mine would do night after night, the others I'd hold, both the living and the dead, the sweat, the love made, the dreams I would have and the streets I can't walk down; he could never have imagined these years, could never have imagined how or why I'd cry to this music, that these songs would be our songs, that these nights could be our nights, but when the lights go down you do imagine, and you must, tonight and tomorrow night and every night of our lives, because that's what we sit in the dark for, that's why we go out at night, because the future has still to happen, the show has still to start, my father is going to have a son, and it will happen, the curtain will rise night after night and so hold my hand and I'll take you there, hold my hand in the dark, hold it, day after day, year after year, night after night after night.

The show ends with an image of the company all turned looking upstage at a glorious sunburst fading slowly to black.

ROYAL COURT WRITERS

The Royal Court Writers series was launched in 1981 to celebrate 25 years of the English Stage Company and 21 years since the publication of the first Methuen Modern Play. Published to coincide with each production, the series fulfils the dual role of programme and playscript.

The Royal Court Writers series includes work by

Karim Alrawi
Thomas Babe
Neil Bartlett
Aphra Behn
Howard Brenton
Jim Cartwright
Anton Chekhov
Caryl Churchill
Sarah Daniels
George Farquhar
John Guare
Iain Heggie
Robert Holman
Ron Hutchinson

Terry Johnson
Manfred Karge
Charlotte Keatley
Paul Kember
Hanif Kureishi
Stephen Lowe
David Mamet
Marlane Mayer
G. F. Newman
Wallace Shawn
Sue Townsend
Timberlake Wertenbaker
Snoo Wilson

METHUEN MODERN PLAYS

include work by

Jean Anouilh
John Arden
Margaretta D'Arcy
Peter Barnes
Brendan Behan
Edward Bond
Bertolt Brecht
Howard Brenton
Jim Cartwright
Caryl Churchill
Noël Coward
Sarah Daniels
Shelagh Delaney
David Edgar
Dario Fo
Michael Frayn
John Guare
Peter Handke
Terry Johnson
Kaufman & Hart
Barrie Keeffe
Larry Kramer
Stephen Lowe

Doug Lucie
John McGrath
David Mamet
Arthur Miller
Mtwa, Ngema & Simon
Tom Murphy
Peter Nichols
Joe Orton
Louise Page
Luigi Pirandello
Stephen Poliakoff
Franca Rame
David Rudkin
Willy Russell
Jean-Paul Sartre
Sam Shepard
Wole Soyinka
C. P. Taylor
Theatre Workshop
Sue Townsend
Timberlake Wertenbaker
Victoria Wood

METHUEN WORLD CLASSICS